My Favorite Color is Red
Experiments with Lines
1999-2005

Derek Fenner

The Positively Past Post-Modern Poet Series #4

BOOTSTRAP PRESS
LOWELL, MASSACHUSETTS

Cover Drawings: "Wallace Berman," by Derek Fenner. 11" x 14" Ink on vellum.

Author drawing: "Me & Robert Downey Jr.," by Derek Fenner. 14" x 17" Pencil, ink and watercolor on paper, 2003.

This book would not be in your hands had it not been for a generous donation from Ray Settle, a southern gentleman. I am personally indebted to Ryan Gallagher for curating this manuscript. Thanks go out to the whole Bootstrap crew, especially Jessica and her assistant Olivia. And a hearty thanks to my proofreaders Tina Brown Celona and John Galvin. Thank you to Gavin Pate and Lisa Jarnot as well for their kind words on this book.

ISBN 0-9711935-5-X

Bootstrap Press Books are designed and edited by Derek Fenner and Ryan Gallagher and published at Bootstrap Productions,82 Wyman Street, Lowell, MA 01852.

THIS IS A BOOTSTRAP PRODUCTION!

This book is dedicated to

my family

Big Ray

&

the boys at S & S Giant Tire in Hooterville, Kentucky.

For Narissa
in admiration,
friendship, & love.

Dan Fa

My

Favorite

Color

is

Red

Table of Contents

Preface

*Man lives by pulses; our organic movements are
such; and the chemical and ethereal agents are
undulatory and alternate; and the mind goes
antagonizing on, and never prospers but by fits.*

Ralph Waldo Emerson "Experience"

Vincent van Gogh, a really great writer of letters, once wrote "The crayon has
a real gypsy soul." Any artist who has had the pleasure of pulling a cadmium
red oil bar down a piece of blanched paper and bending the line of red crayon
debris with a thumb to create an aura of movement and depth may be able to
understand why Derek Fenner writes—to create what cannot be expressed
visually. To stand under a vision and draw its skeleton. To exist in a world of
mathematical shadows and absurd emotions and theory and syndicated sit-
coms and bourbon and blues and blondes.

These experiments in writing read like a collection of day notes, letters, ran-
dom swabs of interesting colors, manifestos, poems, and cacophonous dreams
with quick cuts and ornery characters. Some of these characters will disap-
pear in history due to personal obscurity, some will be immediately recogniz-
able, and most suffer from an American post-modern sort of Byronic doom—
beatific, brooding, and incredibly intelligent. Don't get hung up on the names,
but research them later. They make the universe worth experiencing.

The previous paragraph does not apply, however, to "The Katie Couric Odes",
an absurd experiment which obfuscates the boundaries between performance
art and poetry. In case you wonder when you read these hyperbolic odes—
they were sent as letters to her. There is most certainly a file. Eventually, they
became the basis of Derek's first collage novel where the protagonist, also
named Derek Fenner, writes a local newscaster a series of letters that spell out
an apocalyptic terrorist plot. The fictional Fenner is a modern Polyneices
with an occult knowledge of religion and a propensity to fall in love with
propaganda and "a sublime set of pearly white chompers." The real Fenner is
a neo-Platonist—his search for Eros is the search for the divine, but his Psyche
is strange enough to make Thomas Taylor laugh.

And the mind goes antagonizing on—Humans have never been very success-
ful battling the wild. Embrace it and learn from it. Maybe one day, we will
all be able to fuck Katie Couric. Thoughts like this may land you in jail,
where Derek has worked as an art teacher for the last three years, picking up
on a language at which academics scoff. In the tradition of "documentary
poetics", Derek has immersed himself in the rhythms and grammar of a uniquely
American language—that of our incarcerated youth population. He nails it.
Pops and clicks appear, not as the sound-scape of the Beats experiencing
jazz, but as a death rattle. His essays are existential and touching and tough.
His "Gangsta' Haikus" are street koans and Homeric boasting and lyric code
for life "in-lock". What's the sound of / a Buddhist being plugged in / the
back of the skull?

Read Robert Duncan's essay "Towards an Open Universe", "Beauty strikes
us and may be fearful, as there is a great beauty in each step as Oedipus seeks
the heart of tragedy, his moment of truth, as he tears out his eyes, and sees at
last"—Visit any one of our "correctional facilities", or Cleveland (with your
college degree in hand), and engage in dialogue. Exist outside your comfort
level, then "Fall down on your knees, babe, and pray" because—

"It's a beautiful day for a disaster."

Ryan Gallagher
Lowell, MA
October 2005

A man who collects his poems screws together the boards of his coffin. Those outside will have all the fun, but he is entitled to his last confession.

Basil Bunting

My Favorite Color Is Red, and My Favorite People Are People Who Like Red

I was born in my childhood. I sat in the back of the classroom and yes, I was sent to the principal's office. He told me that I was "a leader of men", but I was leading them in the wrong direction.

I make art and I write about looking. Beauty is what makes you feel good. Beauty and eloquence co-extend with enthusiasm to terrorize the fakes. Art is inanimate. People live. This is an exhibition of space. Our understanding outruns the ordinary usage of words.

My favorite color is red, and my favorite people are people who like red.

I am familiar with the pictures that interest me—pictures that would be unimportant if I saw them as flat symbols, yet they move me as related planes. The history of painting is a history of sight. The bourgeois rule has turned us into savages.

Primordial Lounging Poems

And There Wasn't a Mailbox In Cheyenne
for Allison

Appetites are the basics of being human and we ate grilled cheese sandwiches at the Driftwood Café one Tuesday in February. When I look at these raw materials, machinery and labor, I know that it comes down to Bill telling me to catch the future in less than a second.

Now I know that there are two thousand pictures or more in that second and I will not contend that I am always sure which one tells the truth. They are all inventions. Solitude lies as well.

"Vide cor tuum" said Dante Alighieri and I wonder if he was waiting for my move. Well, I'm making it.

And there wasn't a mailbox in Cheyenne that windy day. They say that the train stops frequently and the wind never. We wrote postcards to each other in a new state and listened to the signs. I told you about Cheri the sculptor without sculpture and you understood the consequences it caused her. You told me a joke that wasn't funny. I was watching you sharp to see if Dave had any truth in his concerns of you being an animal.

Maja desnuda turned into *Maja vestida* and we both felt that Ava Gardner could never pull off that role. You didn't want the whole solar system, just Jupiter. In the Albany Bar and Grille, I searched for the memory of our first night. We met on common ground on the wooden gallery floor in a museum trying to be contemporary. Later that night, I got in trouble for pouring beer the wrong way. You didn't mind that or my mis-buttoned shirt.

In Cheyenne, Wyoming the postal system is screwed up. Melancholy arises when the connections between this world and the divine world of salvation seem to be lost beyond recovery. In Tom Phillips' *Seventh Axiom*, "The post-card creates the site shown in it. After two or three postcards had appeared, Carnaby Street started to become a postcard reproduction of itself."

Postmodernism challenges the old styles with image making techniques based in technology. Don't tell Jonathan Andrews in Cheyenne's only indoor flea market that his calculator is modern though, he'll hike up the price. The definition of Assemblage Art—fragments not intended as art objects. This is where we began. Yet what came before is the foreshadowing. I picked out a light grass green 1930s wool coat with a mink collar for you in the aisle where I heard Susan Sontag's voice,

> *Recall that Breton and the other surrealists who invented the second-hand store as a temple of vanguard taste and upgraded visits to the flea markets into a mode of aesthetic pilgrimage. The surrealist ragpickers' acuity was directed to finding beautiful what other people found ugly or without interest and relevance—bric-a-brac, naïve or pop objects, urban debris.*

If I failed to mention Joseph Cornell and his boxes, I would be doing a great injustice to the foundations of assemblage. Joseph Cornell made these really great boxes just before the West Coast exploded.

On June 14th, 1994 Edward Kienholz was buried on Howe Mountain in his 1940 Packard. Smash, his cremated dog, was in the back seat. Ed had a dollar in his pocket, a bottle of good Italian wine from 1931, and a deck of cards—enough to get him started in the next world.

On Tuesday, February 16th, 1999 around four o'clock in the afternoon, we stood laughing in front of the United States Post Office. We were only looking for blue boxes. The Wrangler Store stood three blocks west. The sun was setting on you and the moon was on its rise.

Cleveland Airport Lounge 3:21 p.m.

for Ryan

Dark and him met west of her (definitively us) like aviation
mobility #16 on list ranks lower than translation
though higher than watching television

And so his sound, later heard tasting
like fresh olives
deeply pitting his mood—Uptight, heady
Plato under disco ball

Gather round the fire caressed by gods

It wasn't something we were supposed to see
The atmosphere above the clouds

In the wake of something else
we learned to live with Pluralism

Primordial Lounging

Wipe your hands across your mouth, and laugh;
The worlds revolve like ancient women
Gathering fuel in vacant lots.

T.S. Eliot

On Saturday, we liked grapes all day long and we never titled it. She said that Ezra Pound's *Cantos* must be out of order. Like Rothko's early work, I felt some form in the content of the day—something with a history, primordial lounging.

Nerves made me question the opportunity of that quick line drawn close. Max Beckmann was mistaken in proclaiming my future. We must believe that the great misery to come has no need for participation in small towns in Indiana.

When she stepped in a shadow of half reflectance toward the window, I saw clear though the moment. I thought of Weston's green pepper—her shoulder in the blanket.

Art Poem

Red shirt, blue shorts	*Jasper Johns*
An analytical temple of a palace of poems	*Ian Hamilton Finlay*
The rape of a big casket	*Edward Kienholz*
Living alone with Loplop	*Max Ernst*
One hears an elegant whisper	*Cy Twombly*
A bird in space	*Constantin Brancrusi*
Rolled wood hangs	*Martin Puryear*
Wipe tears or streams of sweat away	*Jackson Pollock*
It's the third of May	*Francisco Goya*
We are whispers in a theatre	*Eric Fishl*
Pebbles are nature's way	*Henry Moore*
Work stone faces	*Alex Katz*

Diary of a Genius

Swans reflect the poetry
of America. Elephants
are Original Sin.

Mae West, the
great masturbator on the beach
with a telephone.

Salvador! Salvador!
Stop staring
and flush.

"So I fear that I have to follow my desires"; on de Kooning

Following Arshile Gorky, a sinuous taut line. Edge implies volume in a single gesture. Candied greens aquamarines. Hooked re-curved line takes on speed.

Then Rauschenberg erased it. Took him weeks to un-make that drawing. Convinced Willem with a bottle of bourbon—the painting wouldn't suffer. Making another brush stroke brilliant does not matter when the broken mind knows of something better.

Excavation. I have anxiety about falling off a chair in a crowded restaurant.

Meditations on "The Thinker"
for Christian

I.

I'm at work avoiding it by re-reading Dali's genius. *He respectfully put the dish before me.* Everyone else seems actively resistant to new ideas. People are thinking of how to improve their workout program while I try to out-work my mind tonight with a long letter to you. Homespun solutions are not always the answer.

The album is the soundtrack you see—not to the movie. Tonight we will abandon ideas entirely for tooth worms and spider juice. This is not verse set as epigraphs with spaces and soft-returns. It is the New Testament. When I burn a bull on the altar as a sacrifice, I know it creates a pleasing odor for the Lord (Leviathan 1: 9). The problem is my neighbors. They claim the odor is not pleasing to them. Should I smite them? I would like to sell my daughter into slavery as sanctioned in Exodus 21: 7. In this day and age, what do you think would be a fair price for her? Leviathan 25: 44 states that I may indeed possess slaves, both male and female, provided they are purchased from neighboring nations. A friend claims that this applies to Mexicans, but not Canadians. Can you clarify? Why can't I own Canadians? Most of my male friends get their hair trimmed, including the hair around their temples, even though this is expressly forbidden by Leviathan 19: 27. How should they die?

Some men say global managers are made not born. This is not a natural process. We are waiting to jump. Chalk it up to professional enthusiasm. Experiment with local herbs and flowers until you tinker a better system, like a porcelain egg cup.

Dear Pragmatism is not a Beatles tune. REEBOX CEO Paul Fireman is a manager who knows how to profit from THE PUMP. May he make a million shoes. My parents came up with ready-made answers the day that I asked about the scattered dust of stars spread like seeds in the night sky. Purge your diet of buzzwords like like. Judge practical consequences. Tie your (k)nots to the here and now. Get rooted in genuine problems. Get drunk on genuine drafts. Adopt a suit for particular people and situations. Test and refine this suit through active experimentation. Discard all ideas when they are no longer useful. No reason to clutter up the brain. *The next day the stars found themselves driving into the beak of a gigantic peregrine falcon, yellow and mud, until they loomed closer and closer, blue sky vanishing on either side.*

II.

It's time creative types establish if they are different or not. Ironically, this ethic fosters a bureaucratic culture which is supposedly the last bastion protecting us from the encroachment of our American lives. A manager is not a leader. A leader is someone who manages to get by at all costs. I will survive.

Have you heard the story of Dali's first date with the fashionable Gala? Naked in his bedroom with her four flights down ringing the bell, he panicked, covered himself in shit, answered the door and exclaimed—"I think I'll just go change."

My plan was to create an independent pilot operation under the sole direction of the inside of a shingle factory during an explosion—the same factory that the critics claimed caused the ruckus in Marcel's life. This has to do with love in the same way that bumps on your ugly does. If there are children in the room, please turn them up. This is not intended for an adult audience. I'm not the king of Hip-Hop. I'm just trying to be real.

Elegant women have no noses! Portraits of tightly packed figures resemble Max Beckmann's *Deposition*. The spectacle seduces us by endowment of sympathy, for we stand under a bridge wet from the rain windy near the train, carnival green and violent pink. I'm trying to answer all of the questions. The idea is getting support from the bottom. It gets the middle people on the horse faster. I don't think you change a culture. I think you coach people to win. They all want to go home at night and feel that they've made a contribution. Stop all still-life painters with two large candles.

I want to blur the acting (snapping the picture) with the gaining pleasure (seeing the shot). Walk the plank or change. We had it all wrong when we centralized the art into movements and decentralized the paper. Where are you today in the change process?

III.

Those sound suspiciously like marching orders. Lock your doors. Grab your gun. The Restoration has begun. A hand made Kentucky rifle is mounted in the back window of a Ford F-150. Over a thousand miles away, sailboats race on the Delaware. Fifth Avenue faces are unhappy in comparison. The wake of the ferry wrestles water on dock and we all go stag to Sharkey's.

I saw the moon over the mountains, which is not translatable digitally. Landscapes mark children. Streamlines and breadlines. The race for the sky began in 1926 with the Larkin Tower project. High noon, four lane road—Brian exits near Blackhawk. However far from sturdy soil, he wants to be drunk in German. *It is disastrous to name ourselves* Willem de Kooning. Loggerheads over NATO and the Common Market. These are the gritty cities in the age of leftovers. A hand made Kentucky rifle is mounted on ochre and red on red. Recall a world of blacksmiths and railroads.

Alternate Ending (Or What I Wished Happened)

Upon hearing the Hindu dreams, I walk back to the strollers and choose a fine blue one with a flag. Making way towards Monkey Island, I walk out on the bridge and yell to the inmates that their rescue is near. I push the Pepsi machine over the railing and swim toward the island.

The Katie Couric Odes

My words are aphrodisiacs if you say them right.
Tupac Shakur

The $100 Million Woman

My favorite musical is "Kiss Me Katie" and I wish she would be in my company. In her, NBC has a reliable brand; an angel who came from a perky suburban brunette and turned into a burnished blonde power broker. I have fallen in love with her. If I had Katie Couric, I would fill champagne into a million plastic flutes and toast the world. I don't recall anybody being in this much demand since I got here. I would love for Katie to be here so I could ask her: "Katie Couric, will you marry me?" Katie Couric's smile at 44 is always keeping me up at night. In the first moment of waking up, I think about her bangs and her soft voice that calls me to the world. Indeed, she is a siren. Forget about Ann Curry, look at my Katie. I can't believe I said "my Katie", but she is everyday growing sleeker, blonder. With each successive clip, I grow somewhat shell-shocked.

The nightly news is not for Katie. She's the glory in every morning. Who watches the 6:30 p.m. news anchors? They're a bunch of people in adult diapers. Katie Couric wears a red thong for me every morning. When she wakes up, Katie Couric sighs and goes off to work thinking of me. She often rolls her eyes off camera because she knows just how much better she is than Lauer, Roker, and Curry. She carries them all—my Miss Universe, my Katie Couric. She does not mind the age gap. She's fresh. Plus, I'd take her last name. Call me Derek Couric. Call me Mr. Katie Couric. Call me Katie's Boy Toy. Call me anything that has to do with my Katie, my Couric. Thank you Tim Russert for discovering Katie. He knew that she was willing to give the audience what they wanted: Bob Dole and Big Tobacco, O.J. Simpson, George W. Bush. Forget Andy Rooney, he's old and dying. Don't even look to Oprah. World, turn your eyes to Katie Couric. She'll be up front. She'll kick the tires. She'll tell it like it is. Give them hell, Katie Couric. Give them something to talk about. I will never get enough news as long as Katie delivers it. Staring at me, I press the pause button, stare into her eyes, and believe everything she says. I'm mesmerized / hypnotized / synchronized with my Katie Couric, who loves me like the color gold.

The Fantasy Overflows

I start to fear for the world when I think about eternity. When I look out the window after the rain and watch her gallivanting along, I think, damn, love is coming over me. How shall I pass the time? I always say to myself, "Katie Couric deserves a good man." Must be a fine thing— that virtue. Sometimes I hold my breath while thinking about Katie. All is still. She's my beautiful fixed idea, my Eastern dream. Katie's pure for me. With most women, it's like we'll have sex, and afterwards, I'll be glad it's over. It's not like I don't come. But it just stopped there, no matter how much I enjoyed it.

I don't know what else to say about it, except that it would be different if I were with my Katie, my Couric.

I Don't Believe in the Sun

With trees, such cruelty in winter. No shade, or all the time I think of where it went. Usually I feel this pressure of content on the picture of trees, which move back from the memory of fall in Western Kentucky—a simple way of color coming clean on the palette which only a cloudy sky can provide. It's hard to believe in sunny days when there are so many of them. I'm looking out, steering clear of all non-sequiturs, pushing toward a sublime that typifies the beauty of a goodbye party for Katie Couric, whom I just may love enough to put the sun back in its place in the sky. This is only one part of the WE LOVE KATIE marathon, where she comes in glowing, a literal golden girl: all golden hair, creamy golden dress, chunky golden shell necklace, and glossy make-up. My sun, Katie Couric is my sun. "God I feel like my life just flashed before my eyes, not to mention all those really heinous haircuts." I'm having a hard time these days distinguishing the difference between Hollywood, life, and Katie Couric. Katie Couric, who blends all three into one tight golden package, is my solar system distracting me from the work. Desire / Disaster. Katie Couric is at the marriage of scandal. We have only got to look at the sky to escape it. Nothing can be omitted. Experience drunk, experience sober. Compulsions are never civil. In the blondeness of Katie Couric, I find not a cloud in the sky. I realize she's more than just a novelty, my Katie Couric, my sun. I move from her face outward. Yes, once you've seen something, it remains in your memory. With Katie Couric, days pass to night to days beginning again at the end. I'm smitten. I no longer believe in the sun.

The Taste of Beauty

A statue that's ivory grew soft in my hands. I stand amazed, afraid of being mistaken, my joy tempered with doubt and in the sound of her sighs, I hear snow falling. Her beauty, an act of grace, promises everything. Taste is residue of beauty and she tastes like coffee must taste to those people in TV commercials from the eighties—good to the last drop or the first part of waking up. A shake of beauty. She's the way raspberries and mint taste together, the sugarcane of her skin. I want to devour her for a lifetime.

A Lover's Discourse

When I see her, I feel as if God has greeted me and apparently not sent me off to hell. I actually survived. She is the Roman goddess Venus and every bit as Olympian as the show she lives on. My soul, when I embraced her, came to my lips, as if the wretch would leave me and go elsewhere. And her name is Katie Couric and she whispers to me, "My other self, will you answer? At last, I am never tired of you. I want you. I dream of you— for you against me."

Your name is a perfume about me. Colors burst among the thorns. Bring back my heart with cool wine. Make me your morning landscape, for Sappho has said it best, "when I glance at Katie even an instant, I can no longer utter a word: my tongue thickens to a lump, and beneath my skin breaks out a subtle fire: my eyes are blind, my ears filled with humming, and sweat streams down my body, I am seized by a sudden shuddering; I turn greener than grass, and in a moment more, I feel I shall die."

Katie at the Palaz of Hoon

It was the dig
going through layer
after layer, rudiments
in meaning,
or the criticism
of being.
She lives there
to jar her life and
execute the air unseen.

An Ode of Warning

Matt Lauer, you think your enthusiasm is the real thing. I happen to deal well with foreign subjects, but I hate you, with your insertions between the contract and the usage of pure taste. You're all nose, man. Think of it—nothing is certain except disorder and your giant nostrils. In the meantime, a type of hallucination is how I cast a shadow, still trembling regardless of size, on the TV, daring always that the soul fashions the flesh of a thieving bird. I am that vulture. So steer clear of my Katie, my Couric.

How Is Katie Couric In the Sack?

That's like asking a man, hours from sunrise, what it will look like.

The Palm at the End of My Katie

I've fallen madly in love with Katie Couric, and it's not puppy love either. Though sometimes I wish we'd do it doggy style. This would be that real deal kind of love affair. It could outlive a newsflash on the world stage. I feel it coming—the day we meet eye to eye, fall madly in love, and complete the dreams we've already begun.

Her name slides off my tongue like a stamp that is too wet. Does that tell you anything about our love? Katie Couric is poetry and in this poem there are poetics you can feel. And that my friends, is the sober truth of it all—the palm at the end of my Katie / beyond the last thought, rises / in her red thong.

Untitled

And find
in that
the sexual
body intercourse
of is
Katie's just
bosom like
you you.

From Inside These Walls
& Gangsta Haiku

On 40 deuce street,
sold trees, flame to fiends and fame.
Bum rush. Love is straight.

Ah you forced it man—
cuz stays holdin it down.
He's OG for real.

Went gone got PC.
A snitch is a snitch is a
punk dead man walking.

Washington

Alone in his cell, the convict is handed over to himself; in the silence of his passions and of the world that surrounds him, he descends into his conscience, he questions it and feels awakening with him the moral feeling that never entirely perishes in the heart of man.

Michel Foucault Discipline and Punish

Clients shall walk in single file during movement. Clients shall receive permission from staff to move about a location for any reason. All clients and staff shall stop or return to the point of origin if one client needs to stop or return for any reason to the point of origin. All client movement shall cease during client counts to ensure that clients are not counted twice. The use of restraints of clients shall be limited to situations where the client is demonstrating by his/her actions that he/she is dangerous to him/her self or others, and no other intervention has been or is likely to be effective in averting the danger. Clients shall be released from restraint at the first indication that it is safe to do so. If a client dies during a physical restraint, fill out the appropriate forms.

This is a bit of an exaggeration, (but only a bit). I work in a world of policy. The "clients" are boys and girls from the ages of around 9 to upwards of 21 years old. I am their art teacher. They will be the children left behind, even with the implementation of the NO CHILD LEFT BEHIND ACT. These young men and women are serving time for their own safety and for the safety of the public. They are in jail. If you are a parent, close your eyes.

Washington said to me the other day in art class, "Yo D, don't you know it's hard bein from tha slums, eatin five cent gums, not knowin where your next meals is comin from?" Like a lot of my kids, Washington is growing up in *the bricks* (a public housing project) and *in-lock* (jail). In lock, he's safer than on the streets and he knows that he can count on *three hots and a cot*. On the out, things aren't so good. Washington reps a street set affiliated with the Crips. He's a self proclaimed *banger* (gang-member). His favorite color is blue. Wear red around Washington for the wrong reason and he'll "*wild out on yo' punk ass*." He's been with me for just over six months and is awaiting a program placement for violent offenders. Lots of *A&B w/ DW* (Assault and Battery with a Deadly Weapon) on his rap sheet. Like all of us, his story starts much earlier than here.

Washington's father died when he was eight years old. Soon after, Washington began to skip school and spend increasing amounts of time on the streets. He never learned to read or write beyond a third grade level. His mother's new boyfriend moved in with the family and started beating Washington and his mom. Washington started hangin' on the block with an older group of kids. They took to him right away and *beat him in* (initiated him) to their gang. He greatly admired one of the older boys in the gang who had the reputation of an *enforcer* (soldier). He became his protégé.

This is Washington's fourth time in lock. He's considered an *OG* (*Original Gangsta* (one who's *put in work*)). While Washington is in lock, he plays the game well by silently biding his time until he can be re-released back into the wild. He keeps his affiliations silent for the most part. He's a known gang member, so staff usually keeps his enemies off the *unit* (cell block). Sometimes they do slip through the cracks though, and Washington always *gets over* (wins). The first time he was locked up, three rival members came through and jumped him. His nose was broken along with several ribs. When Washington returned from the hospital, he didn't retaliate. He claimed no gang affiliation to staff when they asked why he was jumped. He told them he disrespected one of the boys. He went *PC* (protective custody) and silently planned his revenge. He was a model citizen on the unit, which got him some extra privileges like clean-up duty. The days went by and the other boys figured he was no threat. They eventually got comfortable with his presence. One day, while mopping the laundry room, he found a long four-inch utility nail left behind by a sloppy contractor that morning. He seized the opportunity to exact his revenge. He hid the nail in the mop, knowing that he had the sole clearance to mop for the next day or two. That night, he tore up a t-shirt in his cell and braided strips of it together to make a rope. The following morning, he tied the rope around his waist under his underwear. He waited until dinner to set it. Washington finished his dinner very quickly and asked if he could get a head start on his clean-up duties so he could watch the movie that evening. He got the clearance and went to the mop bucket. He tied one end of his rope to the nail and wrapped the remaining length of it around his fist, letting the nail through his first two fingers. He gained a sight line on those three boys and attacked quickly. He *poked* (stabbed) all three a number of times before he was finally restrained. That story follows Washington everywhere he goes. Kids generally leave him alone. When asked why he did it, he answers, "I got bored."

In art class the other day, I asked Washington what his dream was. He told me that for now, it's to open his own door.

My classes change daily, and throughout any given week I see around 175 juveniles on five units all held in one building—the revolving door of youth crime. My class motto is, *The only freedom you have is the discipline you choose.*

No client shall be restrained for the purpose of punishment or for the convenience of others. No restraint shall include chokeholds, headlocks, full-nelsons, half-nelsons, hog-tying, or the use of pressure points to inflict pain. A 5-point restraint that includes securing of the arms, head, and legs shall not be used as a restraint or as part of the continuum of intervention.

A tight knuckle game.
Chips stacked whips fat dutch sparked—
I'm out on these streets.

Sirens go woop woop—
that's the sound of tha police.
Ears perk on my block.

Like J. Timberlake,
you can cry me a river
cause I fucked your girl.

I stay seein bricks,
buildings numbered one through eight.
I'll never leave here.

Looking for heaven
livin in Hell, I'm gonna
be spittin to death.

G, I done told you,
so don't come at me hyped up.
You know how I do.

Called up my cousin
the other day tryin to
get your brains pushed back.

You've got your kid and
your baby-mama-drama.
I've got Jimmy Hats.

Born inside them bricks
I was gutta way before
Ready to Die hit.

Adams

Estimated number of people who live in a "state of concern": 180,000,000.

Walking the walk and knowing the walk are different. Pop culture tells us that. The form of the prisoner is the form of our unfinished lives. To quote economist Kenneth Arrow: "We must simply act, fully knowing our ignorance of possible consequences." All of us hold the innate possibility of being the prisoner. The juvenile delinquent follows the challenge that Goethe poses at the end of Faust: "In the beginning was the deed." He can think not much further back than that deed which landed him behind bars, inside the walls. Goethe suggests that in the moment of a fatal or flawed decision, engagement precedes knowledge. To know, one must first do. Only from such blindness does insight emerge. Ask Oedipus. Ask any one of my students.

Someone asked me the other day what my goals were in working with locked up kids. I told them to leave my job with the same number of holes in my body that I came in with. He said he could never do what I do. I know I couldn't do what he does. But it got me thinking about what it is I really do after I walk through seven doors each morning to get to my students. I'm not sure I do much more than give them a place to be heard, visually and vocally. It's been a rough month in lock. We've had a number of "group disturbances" (riots) and a lot of gang activity. Numbers are high and as the holidays near, kids become highly stressed and emotional. A lot of them have already found out that they will be locked up for Thanksgiving. This only adds fire to this emotional crucible.

But let's cut to the chase. I'm an artist and I teach art to criminals. So I try to make it fun. What is art? For me, art is play, and this play is one of the most immediate of all experiences. Those who have cultivated the pleasure of play cannot be expected to give it up simply to make a political point or avoid one. Art will *go on,* in somewhat the same sense that breathing, eating, or fucking will go on. Kids like art. Even thugs.

Adams loves my art class. He told me that he likes that I don't conduct class in "Last Word" (silent unless spoken to) and that I play his kind of music. He said it's the only place he can let his guard down and chill cause no one wants to mess up a good thing by setting it on another resident. Adams is 16 years old. He is of Cape Verdean descent and was born and raised in the projects. Recently, his family was able to move into a one-family home. This did not solve their problems. Mom and Dad both work full-time jobs and they try to keep a close eye on Adams and his older sister July. There has been a recent influx of gang-activity in the Cape Verdean community, but because of his parents' interest in his life, Adams had steered clear.

When I first got Adams just under a year ago, he was 15 and brought in on an "Assault and Battery with a Dangerous Weapon with Intent to Murder" rap. I watched his life change from bad to worse to un-fucking believable. Adams is now, at 16, a Youthful Offender and may very well serve a number of years behind adult prison bars, after a three year warm-up stint here in Juvenile Corrections. His charge has changed as well— it has made its way to First-Degree Murder.

Who did he assault and batter? His sister's boyfriend. Who did he kill? His sister's fiancée. This isn't a riddle. Let me explain. Adams was at home on the night of his first arrest, hanging out with his cousin watching *106ʰ and Park* on BET. His sister was upstairs with her boyfriend, Odairson. Adams heard some screaming and assumed they were fucking. July came down stairs bleeding from her side screaming, "He cut me, he fucking cut me!"

Adams and his cousin ran up the stairs and found July's junkie boyfriend blazed and holding a knife, claiming it was an accident. They beat the shit out of him. This wasn't the first time he got high and hurt July, but Adams wanted to make sure that it would be the last. The fight rolled down the stairs and out the front door. Once outside, Adams' father and uncle, who were in the garage, joined him. Adams found a bat and handed it to his dad who used it on Odairson's ribs. There was a lot of screaming and then sirens. Adams' father, uncle, and cousin split. Adams saw his target getting up and grabbed the bloody bat and went at Odairson a little more before being grabbed by the cops and then brought in to my art class the next day.

I remember him that first day, still full of adrenaline and hate and confusion. He refused to do my work and I sent him back to his cell for a cool-out. He was still in the, "What have I done wrong, this fucker stabbed my sister" stage. He would find out later that day that his sister said the stabbing was an accident and that her brother went mad and tried to kill her boyfriend. No one mentioned that Adams had help. Odairson was unconscious in the hospital. This went on for three weeks. If he did not wake up, Adams would be charged with murder. But if he did wake up and chose to forgive Adams and go along with the family's story, Adams would walk. When Odairson opened his eyes, his memory was more than foggy.

Adams got a phone call from his lawyer. His sister's boyfriend was willing to testify that what happened was a misunderstanding. Adams was confused. Then he got to make a call to his family. His sister answered, and said that she was now engaged to Odairson, who looked forward to his return home. Adams told his sister to not bother with dropping any of the charges because he would kill Odairson the moment he saw him. He told his sister to end the engagement or he would plead guilty.

He got out on a Monday and was brought back on a Thursday. He killed Odairson with his father's rifle. Adams became extremely withdrawn during his next few weeks and the night before his sentencing, he had his "revelation". He didn't murder his sister's fiancée, he saved his sister's life. He was a hero, and he intended to tell the judge everything—how Odairson did drugs, fucked other girls, beat him whenever given the opportunity, beat July, and once even threatened Adams' life over a bowl of cereal. He was sure he could win the Judge's sympathy. He returned the next day with a 3 year youth sentence along with a 20 year adult sentence to commence on his 19th birthday.

I've had Adams in class now for a year and have watched him grow a few inches and put on a few pounds from the state food. He works hard at school and is always helping me out in art class. Like most kids his age, he loves to draw cars and tells me that when he gets out he's going to get a fat whip, with 24 inch rims and a drop kit. He says that with good time and such, he should be out of prison by the time he turns thirty. I turned thirty last month. Sophocles said, "pray for no more at all. For what is destined for us mortal men, there is no escape."

Oh let me find out.
Say on dead dogs you're grimy,
I seen you cryin.

Not gonna wild out—
Daddy's gonna get that cash.
Holla at ya boy.

My mans is no snitch.
Twenty-five to L stretched out
and I'm walking free.

I'm throwin them bones.
Trip like that Jigga/Nas shit—
and I'll bust yo face.

Five O's on me, I'm
stayin strapped, forever trapped.
Walkin the block, cocked.

My rhyme is my grime.
Dog, you fuckin with a man.
(My heart needs a hug.)

Strive for the Cheddar,
Kid. Stay up son, the game's done.
She's my wifey yo.

I like it from the
back from the rear between them
cheeks, layin that pipe.

You get shitted on,
shitted on, force fed some red
ripe bullshit in lock.

Jefferson

"The mind, when it reaches its limits, must make a judgment and choose its own conclusions."

Camus

Try to imagine reaching those conclusions inside an 8 x 10 room with white concrete walls, two metal bunks bolted to the wall, and doors that cannot be opened by your own hands. You are told when to shower, eat, sleep, shit, etc… The light switch to your room is outside the door. The lights are never completely out though; a green halogen slips into every corner. Asleep at night, you are not allowed to cover yourself all the way up. "Keep your face out son, show me some skin Mr. So-and-So." The state has just recently frosted your window to the outside for your protection. Deal with your shit while worrying that your court date may get changed, that you may not be allowed to ever go home, that you may get jumped today, that you may never graduate from any kind of school, that your little brother or sister is getting the brunt of the beatings now that you are in lock.

When children are deprived of happiness, they will find happiness in other forms. It is a serious need—a need as final, as inevitable, to the support of human life as sleep. Jefferson was a good kid, caught up in a bad life. Just like that, I've dropped into the past tense. Jefferson is number five for me in just under a year and a half. I've lost three to guns, one to prison for an eternity, and now one to the system—a system that enveloped him for his own safety, a system that made him choose his own conclusion. For Jefferson, this conclusion was to wait for the 15-minute room check around 2:15 a.m. and slip his sheet around his neck, tie it off to the bunk support, and roll over into an endless sleep.

By the time the guards got back around to room B-12, Jefferson had stopped breathing on his own. The guards could not revive him and the paramedics had to breathe for him on the way to his short handcuffed hospital stay, before being released to the county coroner. There was an investigation. Investigations seem to be happening at a far more increasing rate these days. The Department's strip search policy is being looked at in greater detail. They are investigating what could have been done to stop Jefferson from his final attempt to be happy. The public is appalled that we've had 39 attempts this year and this is the first time one of our juveniles has gotten over since 1999, when a young woman hung herself in her room while her roommate's cries for help were ignored by the third shift guards who were too preoccupied with their game of strip poker. The findings of these investigations are usually never much better than grim. It wasn't just a rumor that certain guards were setting up fights on the second shift and taking the kids to an unmonitored room so they could bet on the fights. It was true. And now, as staff are being trained, they actually have to say, "It is not all right to sleep with the clients." The young woman may be eighteen and legal, but she is in your custody and care. P.S., DNA tests are just so damning.

Enduring a lead-
free white room, I put color
around him, now gone.

I will never again tell Jefferson to stop being so goofy. This was his only crime, he was a cut-up in class. You may wonder why he was locked up. His mother was an addict, his father a pervert, and grandma had just passed away. At fifteen, you don't realize that there is still time for things to get better. Your life is right now and not a moment longer. Jefferson would have been released the day after his suicide to an open program, where he would await adoption, which would probably never happen.

I can imagine the final meeting with his clinician.

"But why can't I go home to my family?"

"Jefferson, your family is not good for you. I know that is hard to understand, but you will see that we are trying to help you. You'll like the program, there are a lot of kids that you can identify with there."

"You mean homeless."

"No, Jefferson, you are not homeless. You will have a nice time there. You just have to give it a chance. Aren't you tired of being locked up here?"

"It's better to think I'm going home than to know that I'm not. When I go to the program, then I'll know I'm never going home. My mom needs me."

"I know Jefferson, I know."

"No you don't, no you don't."

I was interrogated about my dealings with Jefferson the day of his suicide. Did I notice any sort of depression? Come on, the kid was locked up, of course he was depressed. Did I notice any sort of clues? Is there anything I could have done to prevent his death? Sure, I could have been there for him. But I was at home in bed. That is not in my job description.

I went to Jefferson's funeral. I was the only white person there. The family asked that no one from the Department show up, but the chaplain told me that he thought I should go if I felt up to it. I didn't feel up to it, but I went, because Jefferson is different from all the other funeral invitations I get. Jefferson wasn't connected to street violence. Jefferson was just getting by. Jefferson never made gangsta art of raps, whips, and stunts (guns, cars, and easy women). His art was different and I thought his family should have it. When I went up to the casket, among his few childhood pictures, I placed his finest piece of art to date, made just two weeks prior to the most violent thing he would ever do. I can't tell you how strange it was to see his family grieving—to see the mother there in all her glory, the martyr, the afflicted, the addicted. How the community just swarmed over how awful it was, how the Department was to blame.

I bought a frame for his sketch on the way. It was a picture consisting of an equation. On one side of an addition symbol was a picture of the world and on the other was a picture of the 1960's sign for peace. Then an equals sign and a single blue tear with the red circle and a slash through it. The lesson for the day was to draw fear. Jefferson said, "D, I ain't scared of this, I'm scared my little brother will grow up in a world of tears."

I teach art. When I started this job, I never thought I'd be faced with so much death. Now that I am locked up with the kids five days a week, I can begin to empathize a little, to understand how one can just give up. Jefferson's story will not be the saddest. There are slower kinds of suicide going on inside these walls as well.

The preceding merely defines a way of thinking. But the point is to live.
                                                                    Camus

Hittin dem silk sheets.
I stunted her. Rocked her world,
then hit it again.

It's us versus them
On these streets the strong survive
and the weak just die.

We gotta "SQUAD UP!"
Train to keep our game on point,
so the team will rise.

This is thug romance—
I throw her my Champ hoody,
She throws up my set.

She got my name on
her tee, and if the shit hits
the fan, she will squeeze.

The last shall be last.
But on the block we still pray,
the last shall be first.

Snitches be getting
less time yo, not stitches, though
they won't tell you so.

Met this Ace Deuce kid
on 12th street in Mattappan.
Young G boned out quick.

You claim everywhere.
A fucked up set-jumpin-bitch,
you a hood-hopper.

I Stopped Going to Wakes

I stopped going to wakes
a few bodies ago.

Why them bullets, that knife, that syringe have to hit that child?

Don't make me put your heart in your lap, reader, it gets much worse.

Some are born to fail. Others have it thrust upon them.

Inside these walls we are no longer blind to the ways of mankind. Two months ago, I lost three kids in twenty minutes. Leaving the corner store at two o'clock in the afternoon, one was shot in the face: instant death. One shot in the neck: death in 7 minutes. One shot in the back, the leg, and the shoulder: death in 19 minutes. One of these three killed a boy just two nights before for "mean-muggin'" him. Another one of the three just got out from my art class that day. He was in for participation in the gang-rape of a twelve year old girl in the basement of an apartment building. The third was legend in the hood for selling the hottest dope. Story has it he served his own mother the dope she OD'd on.

This shit is serious. Walking past Lil' B's cell today I heard him rashin,

>*I pack a four-five*
>*Hustl'-a-blunt*
>*I get high*
>*and don't give a fuck if I die!*
>*'Cause my son is alive*
>*I grew up doin' dumb shit*
>*that made me wise*
>*Could've died ten times*
>*Baby that made me live*
>*I'd sell my soul*
>*not for no cars or no gold*
>*I been through it / cause my scars is old*

Imagine being locked up inside any situation. Imagine something you or I can't feel, like never going on a vacation. Life to you is devastating. Your fucked up relatives are gone and you're only left with regret. You've got two names, one from the government, one from your family. Names like Man, Ant-Black, Pooh, Snook, Snub, Ace, Sauce, Red, Country, Big-City, Sniper, BG, OG, Big Guy, Little Ty, Spy, Spider, Lil' Shorty, and Tiny.

Some quick shout outs:

I want to take a moment to thank M's mother for making her 15-year-old daughter nurse her younger brother so she could continue shooting up.

Thanks for the HIV infected, herpes infected, and three cases of aggravated rape on a child under 10. Thank you for introducing him into the job market at the age of 6 by pimping him out to pedophiles.

Thank-you for allowing him to get his sister pregnant because you thought it would be hot to have your two lovely children conceive in front of a camera, just in case there was a fetish for a 14-year-old boy on a 29-year-old sister. It's a good thing you sprinkle coke on her food every day to help her stay skinny, especially when the camera adds ten pounds. You must certainly be proud.

Thanks for your son, who is painting portraits of himself in various poses inside a casket. He's doing all of this under a metal bunk on the floor. You see, he won't leave his cell, and he is on a hunger strike and only speaks in the pictures he draws. We've spent two days trying to get him out from under his bunk. The smell is getting worse from his piss and shit. Now he is going to be force fed through a tube while he is chained down to a bed. Honey, don't worry about sending flowers. The state will take care of that too. I know you are worried about your son being placed in an abusive foster home, but we promise we will do our best. He probably won't even be placed for some time, since he's got a lot of time to do in jail, and then we might release him to the Department of Mental Health for a while. By the time he's ready for such a placement, he will only have to endure such abuse for a month or two before he turns eighteen and will be able to return to your loving home.

I love where I work and I love these kids. I just get a little world weary. No matter what they did to arrive in my art class, I try to let them kick back for an hour and try to forget what horrible secrets and crimes their files may hold. We hang on to the lines we draw and the dreams we build in pictures.

I always know when I look tired because they tell me. They let me know when it's time to buy some new shoes, because mine are to the meat. They tell me all the time that art is their favorite subject. I try to understand them by learning their language, listening to their music, and even correcting them when they quote Tupac wrong. They love when I can rash with them, let them know I'm trying every day to understand them a little more. We laugh as much as possible. I tell them about the set I rep. "A-R-T for life Baby! (I rep all the colors.)" They've got me cooking Thanksgiving dinner for them in a couple of weeks. "And none of that dry-ass turkey D. We want that good shit—that Pilgrim/Indian shit, the works you know, mashed potatoes and gravy and something sweet for dessert."

You gets further with
a gun and some kind words than
with kind words alone.

Mojo. Nothing. Punk
motherfucker I blanged your
mans into the ground.

Yo motherfucker,
holla at me and get served
like christmas turkey.

Mad street sets gather.
Pay respect in black *Dickies,*
their Dawg in heaven.

Listen man read my
motherfucking mind. Like church,
we're mass on yo ass.

The Cleveland Sonnets

For the people of Cleveland who've suffered for so many years.

Dear Ryan,

There has never been enough to go around. The right questions aren't asked. Answers never appear. Our words get lost, they wander relentlessly for years before they resurface and make an impression. This is a story of Cleveland. I've returned here from life further east, where you must be enjoying some reading and the wait to become a father.

I'm working in Eastlake at TKP Auto Sales and at Tony's house in Willoughby Hills, "where the city meets the country." I could have said, "where the city meets the sky," and then the rent became whisky. Any off-time from the construction work is spent on the car lot, which feeds me a large surplus of strange characters, and I am almost certain that I will base my second novel on its surreal universe of shysters, down and outs, and pure schizophrenics. (Working title is "The Lot"). I have a new favorite bumper sticker, "HONK IF YOU'RE LONELY".

The bars in Eastlake are the kind I love—big handled bottles of booze that get emptied quick by a local selection of workers and non-workers, whose lives entwine in a number of disgusting and sometimes tragic ways. I met this man who was fucking his brother's sister-in-law, who had three kids. He loved going to the little league games to sit behind her and her husband and think about how hard he fucked her earlier that day, and about the panties she was wearing. This guy used the word "man" too much, but in its repetition it became hypnotic, pinning me against the reflection of myself in the bourbon in front of me. "I'll tell you what Man, I gotta believe there's something better than this man, know what I mean? Man, I'll know her when I see her, see man, reason I'm here man, is cause I gotta pick up a couple under the table jobs. Shit Man, I'll do anything for fifty bucks man, cause that's fifty bucks the old lady doesn't know about man. And I can take it to the bar and meet my future girlfriend. I screw both kinds of women man, pretty and pretty ugly."

The only food to be had here is deviled eggs, pickles, bags of pretzels, and Andy Capp Hot Fries. You know the place—clapboard shacks with names like "The Stumble Inn" or "Bob and Peg's Handle Bar II" and my favorite "Robinhood's Den." They rest right there on Vine Street in Eastlake, nestled among the used car lots, Kmarts, and strip malls. I went to a strip club in the

Flats with Brad and this guy Bruno called "The Champagne Room" and Brandee, young and from Elyria, who was dumb as shit, was my date for an hour while Brad got a brunette named Doll Ray and then Bruno got kicked out of "The Champagne Room" for being too rough with Deanna. It's raining hard outside this life and probably in the city of Cleveland too. I took one day off this whole month. I walked into a hailstorm here with things to do and no time left to do them. Manic spurts of rain.

Anyway, I decided to take the day off, write some letters and draw and read and listen to some music. The nights in Cleveland are often as lonely as a broom, so I scratch notes in the margins of a tattered copy of *Plum Smash* and tell the bartender to set up the bar. Sometimes loneliness is a joke, as long as you have a steady surplus of paints and a city of words and images to build. It's a feeling we crave every now and again, like melancholy—the way people want to see sad movies and go about their sad lives and sometimes get completely shit-faced.

Points and grace,

Derek

One

All the news that's fit to print
isn't in Cleveland Ohio. In fact,
there's not much here like in Flint
Michigan, the universe is trashed.
I mean to tell you how it is.
It's five o'clock and I can't sleep so
I mill around on linoleum steps
replacing insulation in the walls.
It's funny how unhappy people can get
and how god damn ugly too, losing
what once made them feel free.
Deep shit tends to sweeten dreams.
This is how it is when your TV's
old and the color's fucked.

Two

Cleveland, you are ugly in love.
Like the bottomless cup of coffee at the Cracker Barrel,
you make me want to crap. It's seven so it's five hours
before I will throw up from this foul beer baiting.
Bellied up to a lot of bars, these days I'm mindfucked.
You've got me in your grasp. Promises end up broken.
If this continues for much longer, I may need a soul.
Oh Cleveland, you are a soul taker.
So laugh at yourself, little city.
Those who can't don't last a minute
in the game of lasting a minute. Have sex
with yourself and bandage the wounds that
you inflict on boys in the basement longing to get into
your skin clubs, exhaling their youthful exuberance.

Three

Cleveland, why must you turn everything brown
and orange? You ain't ever gonna win the game.
Hell Cleveland, you don't even know the coach's name.
I don't know how to make you famous.
Pathos-weak town—the river runs
puke-like and pungent. Bad coffee
creamer in your eyes. You're spun
out on bar whiskey while I weed
TKP Auto Sales looking for diamond
sutras instead of digging up vacancy signs
for more thorns to grow. All the years
of searching and you are not sympathetic,
just pathetic. So slap the left side of my face—
Cleveland, you've always put me in my place.

Four

My god how you stink in the sun-
shine—this crazy fucking land—leave
my name out of your mouth. I am
Derek "fo' real" and today when I drove a flatbed
truck down Vine Street, nothing happened again.
I got to the lot, slipped on oil that Lee spilt, said "Shit
mother-fucker!" Why can't I fall in love with you,
Cleveland? You really are nasty—you beat me
off in the most abrasive ways—with sandpaper
on my nipples, I've lost all reason. "God is dead"
said Nietzsche and "Nietzsche is God" say the dead.
Forget both and lose all your dirty secrets
at once. Even if I get my shit together—
Cleveland, you can't have me.

Five

Good morning Cleveland. How was your night?
Mine was god damn dreadful. I mean that. My heart aches,
but your discount drug marts could never begin to fill me.
You are in Ohio. It's a beautiful day for a disaster.
Blind me with your #3 and #88 NASCAR bumper stickers.
You could stand to drop a few pounds too. Sit down,
turn your neon lights all the way up. The sun's never coming out,
but at least you have Frisco Freddie's Oktoberfest all year long.
Every Sunday at the Christ Lutheran Church,
its ugly congregation asks "why is life so unfair?"
There's really no difference to you
between the pronunciation of terrorist and tourist.
You make the best of both, Cleveland. Could I be
your next detainee "sittin' on Guantanamo Bay"?

Six

Cleveland, I've given you all my problems and now you've
turned right around and given them back. Sold me out
to the Gold Star Pawn Shop, Inc. I don't want treats
by Pat, so give me the consolation prize once more and I'll
never again step foot in your Imperial Super Buffet.
There's this passage I have memorized from the Bible.
It goes, "Now Cleveland was corrupt
in God's sight, and Cleveland was filled with violence. And God
saw Cleveland, and it was corrupt. For all its dwellers
had corrupted their way upon the city." It's in Genesis.
Find out what's coming your way. God's
gonna get down on you. d.a. levy said
"Somewhere over the rainbow, there's another dump like this.
I know, I know it sounds untrue, but there is, there is."

Seven

Things I Drove in Cleveland

A Cub Cadet riding lawn mower and a Pontiac Grand Prix with T-tops.
A Volvo, a Jeep Grand Cherokee, and a Suzuki Four Wheeler.
A Chevy Blazer, a new Trailblazer, and a Toyota
Avalon after I drove the Buick Le Sabre but not before
I drove the Dodge Neon or the Daewoo Lanos. The Mercedes
was nice and so was the Corvette, but Cleveland is better from a
Ford F-550 flatbed tow truck, or a Ford F-150—maybe
you'd prefer the Kia Sephia or the Isuzu Rodeo?
Maybe you've never driven a GMC Cargo Van or the awesome
V8 Dodge Ram with a lot of get up and go but no knee room.
Listen man, I'll repo' your sweetest dreams if you give me the chance.
I'll take your Grand Prix, Aerostar, Safari, Ranger, and Le Sabre.
Just make your weekly payments you motherfucker.
And just so you know, TKP stands for taking care of people.

Eight

I'd get a new lease on life,
but you're like a slumlord so
I draw out your name in the air—
the dirty smog-filled air.
I dodge seagull shit. Please
quit driving on the bike paths.
It's five o'clock somewhere
and I ain't had a day off in a year.
I'm sick of your imaginary girlfriends,
your Teflon-taped and leaky faucets,
loaning you ten dollars for gas
because your boss never showed up.
The paperboy is in camouflage again
on his way to the *Just One More Tavern*.

Nine

I butchered my dreams the day I stepped out of the car and into a "Cleveland
Steamer". Like any desperate man, that's the way things are here, so I do
what I do and seek solace in a new nickname—
maybe Derek "Longpants". I'm tripping over your dollar
stores with a pocket full of quarters, like a giant
in the *Leisuretime Warehouse*.
I swear to God Cleveland, you're gonna push me till I snap.
(And you should never push a man till he snaps.)
So take me to the *Seaway
Lounge*, I'd like to shoot the bull with the rest of you
and find out how to cope with this shit you call life
in Northeast Ohio. Dust my feathers with disaster.
Feel this ghostly breath on your back. I'll be gone,
but not forever. So I fall down on my knees babe, and pray.

Ten

Cleveland, I can count the number of STDs you've given me
on one hand. Itching, strained—I'm all worn out. Here comes
midnight Mama. You've done it to me again.
You've got me in a tight spot. One day, I'll leave
this loneliness when the night is gone.
It's been a long time and it's hard doing anything.
I'm still trying—it didn't used to be so hard.
I can feel you leaning in on me.
Don't you know it's lonesome sleeping all by myself
when the one I love is sleeping with someone else?
If only you could only leave Ohio, Cleveland, you and I
could be somewhere, anywhere, better than this bad luck lullaby.
I would holler murder, but this freaking town's too small. Cleveland,
you know I'd love you at Giuseppe's Donuts each and every morning.

At Lisa's

I.

You can almost hear the streets of Walnut
Grove from the four-story walk up. Voices
with great songs, "perhaps some day we'll
have another newspaper, one that
tells the truth."

The neighbors' air-conditioned rooms
hum as the lights go
dim in apartment #14.
Harry the Cat, a.k.a Beanhead,
Hair the Bear, Mr. King of 14,
Hare Krishna, Harry He Who
Drinks From My Glass—

A tumbleweed of fine clean cat
hair rolls by at 6 a.m. with a wake-up howl
and if you look right at him
when he speaks
he may just say

I'm just trying to be funny.
I wish you'd stick to the business of Engels
pointing out the relation between machine and thought.

I get up,
feed the Hair Man,
and start the coffee,
return to bed while it brews,
listen to Lisa's new disc.

Caught between the dimensions
of an uptown / downtown
marketplace of chinchilla
like Dylan in his religious years.

I write an essay assembling like them:
Berman, Herms, Conner, Jess, even Ed Kienholz.
Other pictures stare at me—
Tae-wol, Lisa at the sea, and Anselm Hollo
through glass. A painting with two eyes—

I move closer to discuss it.
Deb's painting
goes the way
of a Guston fucking a Klee,
a map in the shadows of light,
rich in philosophical resonance,
physically temporal.

I've been told my whole life to confess.
On the other hand,
I can't imagine why
someone else writes
yours truly when
I'm caught on fire.

Two nights of sweating sleepless fits,
I write on the roof by candlelight—
rough cuts like Dracula must have been written,

a siren and I   go

to check on Harry
behind the Pound books.

II.

Life is just a series of days that fade away. Maybe I'll be here tomorrow. The memory of eternity in the service of midnight—madness, madness, the one I did not expect. At Lisa's, I'm quite happy in this fourth dimension—imagination. At Lisa's, I sleep and wake well. The word and the image become one. I assume that I can put order into the chaos that constitutes the infinite and shapeless void of being. We must not analyze, but create the work of our lives with the same intensity that drives the thickness of our soul.

To let oneself be thrown by things. To bring back our gaze from the distance.

III.

creased

in black

immersed in white

a burst of white

a dread of one single end

what passes sheds light on passage

in the book

no point of origin

Ants! That's what they are Harry!

light

light

to be forgotten by death

One Hundred People You Should Know

A Note On The Process

These are not lithographs, screen-prints, or woodcuts. They are ink portraits. Though they are drawn and assembled from a rather lengthy process, they should yield the impression that they are made very quickly or at least have the scent of technology.

First I find a photograph of the subject that I like; I've always been concerned with how painting has been influenced by photography and vice versa. I am, of course, deeply indebted to the photographers of any picture I use. I make a black and white photocopy of the photograph to simplify the image; one can do the same thing by squinting at a black and white portrait under a very strong light.

I make a few minor notations on vellum in light pencil. I then draw the photograph as if I was going to do a "realistic portrait," but I don't typically shade much beyond two degrees. I pay special attention to the darkest lines. Once I have a drawing that resembles the photograph, I begin making connections and simplifying the image with a lacquer-coated graphite pencil, continuing to make notations while squinting. This technique allows me to break the image down to as few marks as possible. I then erase the pencil markings with kneaded rubber so I am left with a topographical study of the photograph. This sort of chiaroscuro, less violent than a Rauschenberg erasing, helps shape however the lines must move to create a portrait. With a very fine piece of sandpaper, I scuff the graphite lines so that I can better control the ink. Eventually, the portrait appears. I find that each portrait takes between four and six hours. I'm sure I could make them in under an hour with today's technology. I wanted to return to drawing after a number of years and I wanted to make an art book that I could afford to print. After I completed a portrait, I found that it pulled me further into the work of that particular artist or writer. I like to view this book, with quotations on facing pages, as a collection of the hundred greatest influences on my artistic and personal existence in this absurd universe. I hope you make your own list and that it is different from mine. I have structured the order of these hundred people as memoir. Consider it the only way I could imagine presenting a personal essay. These are one hundred people you should know.

Rembrandt van Rijn

My Lord, hang this piece in a strong light and so that one can stand at a distance from it, then it will sparkle at its best.

Gerson, Horst. Rembrandt Paintings. Amsterdam: Reynal and Company, 1968. p. 52.

Grandpa (Jack Fenner Sr.)

Happy Birthday, I hope you have another.

Fenner, Jack. "Overheard". Various locations: 1973-present.

Ted Berrigan

I'll tell you what to do while you're waiting for the bus. When the bus comes, you're on your own. You're gonna have to drive that bus, you might even be that bus, you'll also be all the passengers, and then you're gonna run into your self coming the other way. But you'll take care of that.

Berrigan, Ted. "From a lecture at The Kerouac School of Disembodied Poetics". Boulder, CO.

Anselm Hollo

4

the stuff of the psyche is a smoke-like substance
says Heraclitus it is constantly in motion
only movement can know movement ah
this be head-sensitive material
forever in deep shade
we get together to make noises at each other
when we're not there we miss those noises
but hey boss isn't it time to lighten up says archy
you old opsimath you what's that it's one who learns
things late in life & when has it not been
'late in life,' si vales bene est ego veleo
beloved beasts open to many
'interpretations' we or awe, as in aw shucks
if you are well that is good I am well too

Heraclitus quotes, here as elsewhere, from Guy Davenport's
translation. archy: Don Marquis' vers-libertarian cockroach.

Hollo, Anselm. rue Wilson Monday. Albuquerque: La Alameda Press, 2000. p. 18.

Salvador Dali

Each time someone dies, it is Jules Verne's fault. He is responsible for the desire for interplanetary voyages, good only for boy scouts or for amateur underwater fishermen. If the fabulous sums wasted on these conquests were spent on biological research, nobody on our planet would die anymore. Therefore, I repeat, each time somebody dies, it is Jules Verne's fault.

Dali, Salvador. Dali by Dali. trans. Eleanor R. Moorse. New York: Harry N. Abrams, Inc., 1970. p. 136.

d.a. levy

Red Lady could separate the freaks from the lonely with her eyes closed on a busy street but there were times of agony when even she couldn't touch the coiled fires within some of her children and she cursed the world that had crippled them with unwritten, venomous paths & then there were accidents she never regretted, inquisitors who stumbled in their own blindness (foto of J Edgar Hoover) psychic eunuchs with pale dreams cluttering up the roads she had opened eons before left her laughing, she pushed them into each other and watched them compliment each other on another satori, another 'experience'—it was sad sometimes, but she collected the scarlet seconds between her thighs—she knew she was forever & the day would come when the others would understand her ways and leave her alone to fulfill her own destiny.

levy, d.a. Red Lady. Cleveland: Open Skull Press, 1970. p. 6.

Allen Ginsberg

it was the racks and these on the racks I saw naked in electric
     light the night before I quit,
the racks were created to hang our possessions, to keep us together,
     a temporary shift in space,
God's only way of building the rickety structure of Time,
to hold the bags to send on the roads, to carry our luggage from
     place to place
looking for a bus to ride us back home to Eternity where the heart
     was left and farewell tears began.

Ginsberg, Allen. "In The Baggage Room At Greyhound". <u>Howl</u>. San Francisco: City Lights Books, 1956. pp. 46-47.

Philip Lamantia

To this vast ring of the rising crystal
To swim into mantra rays
Mentation of the vowel
To the sonatal leap
Hidden on the verge of the verbal jungle
A tarantula
Quaintly with a diffidence of speed
Retreats back into its hollow

On this road flexing muscular sinews
The stoned expressions of buddhas crack in their
   sediments
The anteater ways I stumble on
A panther lady on the fleeting disk
Words tumble
On the stretcher bearer's static muse

Lamantia, Philip. "Red Wood Highway". Becoming Visible. San Francisco: City Lights Books, 1981. p.18.

Joe Brainard

I remember when I thought that if you did anything bad, policemen would put you in jail.

I remember on a very cold and black night on the beach alone with Frank O'Hara. He ran into the ocean naked and it scared me to death.

I remember lightning.

I remember wild red poppies in Italy.

I remember selling blood every three months on Second Avenue.

Brainard, Joe. "I Remember". The Angel Hair Anthology. eds. Anne Waldman and Lewis Warsh. New York: Granary Books, 2001. p. 335.

Man Ray

You know, *I'm* not Marcel Duchamp, I'm Man Ray.

Ray, Man. <u>Self-Portrait</u>. New York: A Bulfinch Press Book, 1998. p. 314.

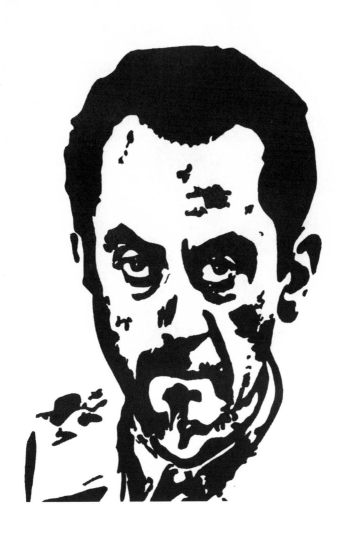

Marcel Duchamp

Dear Stieglitz,

Even a few words I don't feel like writing. You know exactly how I feel about photography. I would like to see it make people despise painting until something else will make photography unbearable. There we are.

Affectueusement,

Marcel Duchamp
(N.Y., May 22, 1922)

Duve, Thierry de. <u>Kant After Duchamp</u>. Cambridge: The MIT Press, 1996. p. 140.

Michael McClure

At the window I look into the blue-gray
gloom of dreariness.
I am warm. Into the dragon of space.
I stare into clouds seeing
their misty convolutions.

The whirls of vapor
I will small clouds out of existence.
They become fish devouring each other.
And change like Dante's holy spirits
becoming an osprey frozen skyhigh
to challenge me.

McClure, Michael. "Peyote Poem". Semina 3. ed. Wallace Berman. San Francisco: Wallace Berman's Semina, 1958.

Michael Gizzi

O ROOSTER OF MAY, dear mailbox, kind sirens who giveth men the goatees to excuse their afterwrath—bless our little electrolytes. The princess inside Salvador Dali's formaldehyde did not invent pornography.

Gizzi, Michael. My Terza Rima. Great Barrington, MA: The Figures, 2001. p.68.

Blaise Cendrars

My pen is frisky

Beat it!

Cendrars, Blaise. "F.I.A.T". <u>Complete Poems</u>. trans. Ron Padgett. Berkeley: University of California Press, 1992. p. 72.

Christopher Smart

For I rejoice like the worm in the rain in him that cherishes and from him that tramples.

Smart, Christopher. <u>Jubilate Agno</u>. ed. W.H. Bond. Cambridge: Harvard University Press, 1954. p. 47.

Lisa Jarnot

dogs are loyal
but

consider painting
circles,

first a round one,
then

the faith-
fullness of
machine gun
fire—

give
Helen
back,

or some other
kind of mission

Jarnot, Lisa. Some Other Kind of Mission. Providence, RI: Burning Deck Books, 1996. p. 27.

Frank O'Hara

You are worried that you don't write?
Don't be. It's the tribute of the air that
your paintings don't just let go
of you. And what poet ever sat down
in front of a Titian, pulled out
his versifying tablet and began
to drone? Don't complain, my dear,
You do what I can only name.

O'Hara, Frank. "To Larry Rivers". The Collected Poems of Frank O'Hara. ed. Donald Allen. Berkeley, CA: The University of California Press, 1995. p. 128.

Larry Rivers

For me, Frank's death is the beginning of tragedy. My first experience with loss. I feel lonely.

Rivers, Larry. <u>What Did I Do? the Unauthorized Auotbiography of Larry Rivers</u>. with Arnold Weinstein. New York: Harper Collins, 1992. p. 465.

Jeni Olin

An infinity begins and backfires—
A stately bang against the universe
Crude and seminal like the Special Olympics
Or the heroine's false sense of invincibility—I just
Want to grab her by her anorectic shoulders & moan
I know, I know, but Snow White she seems so easy
One kiss & she really "came to life." Slut.
I guess I was expecting rain, suspecting
Larry when he was being so good.

Olin, Jeni. "The Para-Olympic Legacy". <u>Blue Collar Holiday & A Valentine to Frank O'Hara</u>. Brooklyn: Hanging Loose Press, 2005. p.15.

Cedar Sigo

There are white roses with
Their leaves and they are
Trapped in the ceilings.
I'm feeling quite sane
Not young again. I had wanted
To see my pages in the dark
He begs me to please
Keep still in the dark.

Sigo, Cedar. <u>Selected Writings</u>. Brooklyn: Ugly Duckling Presse, 2005. p. 27.

Edward Hopper

What I wanted to do was to paint sunlight on the side of a house.

Gerard Malanga

Nobody knows the moment when the eye
Dropper is needed.
There are rumors of noise without reason and in my mind
There are names and living faces.
The young girl sets up love against
Life in the small room that the dead
Dream of the low-living share.
We are not sad together.
Sometimes I don't see you
Behind me. Fatigue of relaxing will
Assume the break
Down where they sit, not saying a word.
There is a world of things
To do in the rising sun
Light when we rub our eyes.
I walk with you. I stop
You are young.
"Trembling I hang by a thread;
I cease to exist if no one thinks of me," you said.

Malanga, Gerard. "Drugs and Cosmetics". No Respect. Santa Rosa, CA: Black Sparrow Press, 2001. pp. 67-68.

H.D.

My sign-posts are not yours, but if I blaze my own trail, it may help to give you confidence and urge you to get out of the murky, dead, old, thousand-times explored old world, the dead world of overworked emotions and thoughts.

Doolittle, Hilda. <u>Notes on Thought and Vision</u>. San Francisco: City Lights Books, 1992. p. 24.

Jack Spicer

Surrealism

Whatever belongs in the circle is in the circle
They
Raise hands.
Death-defying trapeze artists on one zodiac, the Queen of
  Spades, the Ace of Hearts, the nine of Diamonds, the whole
  deck of cards
Promise to whatever is promised
Love to whatever is loved
Ghosts to whatever is ghosts
In our mouths
Their mouths
There is
Hope.

Poe predicted the whole Civil War.

Spicer, Jack. The Collected Books of Jack Spicer. ed. Robin Blaser. Santa Rosa, CA: Black Sparrow Press, 1975. p. 141.

Bernadette Mayer

Booze Turns Men Into Women

Mayer, Bernadette. "Table of Contents". <u>Scarlet Tanager</u>. New York: New Directions Books, 2005.

Robert Duncan

to put down the rage of revolt with *Love, Sweet Love*, she cries

> from the center of terror
> that is the still eye of the storm in her:

"There comes a time when only Anger is Love."

Duncan, Robert. "Santa Cruz Propositions". <u>Ground Work: Before the War</u>. New York: New Directions Books, 1984. p. 46.

Jess (Collins)

One of the things that I've always loved about living in this old house are the water stains and cracks in the ceilings and walls. I can't help staring at them and making pictures or fantasy images out of them. This is what da Vinci said an artist must do—to take note of all stains on the walls and pay particular attention to foliage, things that are very real in an abstract way.

Auping, Michael. Jess: A Grand Collage 1951-1993. Buffalo: The Buffalo Fine Arts Academy, 1993. p. 21.

Tom Phillips

Implicit in that stain right from the start
was all I've since invented and called Art.

Phillips, Tom. <u>Works and Texts</u>. New York: Thames and Hudson, 1992. p. 29.

Francis Bacon

What I want to do is to distort the thing far beyond the appearance, but in the distortion to bring it back to a recording of the appearance.

Bacon, Francis. <u>Francis Bacon: Interviewed by David Sylvester</u>. New York: Pantheon Books, 1975. p. 40.

Joel-Peter Witkin

It happened on a Sunday when my mother was escorting my twin brother and myself down the steps of the tenement where we lived. We were going to church. While walking down the hallway to the entrance of the building, we heard an incredible crash mixed with screaming and cries for help. An awful accident had taken place involving three cars, all with families in them. Somehow, in the confusion, I was no longer holding my mother's hand. At the place where I stood at the curb, I could see something rolling from one of the overturned cars. It stopped at the curb where I stood. It was the head of a little girl. I bent down to touch the face, to speak to it – but before I could touch it – someone carried me away.

Witkin, Joel-Peter. Joel-Peter Witkin: Forty Photographs. San Francisco: San Francisco Museum of Modern Art, 1985.

Michel Foucault

Do not ask who I am and do not ask me to remain the same: leave it to our bureaucrats and our police to see that our papers are in order. At least spare us their morality when we write.

Foucault, Michel. The Archeology of Knowledge. trans. A.M. Sheridan Smith. New York: Pantheon Books, 1972. p. 17.

Antonin Artaud

I am human by my hands and my feet, my guts, my meat heart, my stomach whose knots fasten me to the rot of life.

Artaud, Antonin. "Fragments of A Journal in Hell". Artaud Anthology. trans. David Rattray. ed. Jack Hirschman. San Francisco: City Lights Books, 1965. p. 44.

Will Christopher Baer

I can hear the freeway, the rush and hiss of a thousand cars. The edge, I am coming to the edge of something and I wonder if I am near the ocean and now I raise my eyes to see the curved freeway overpass like the massive spinal column of conjoined twins and glowing against black sky are the big green signs that provide blunt directions to Chinatown and North Beach and suddenly I am scared of the government and I want to get inside.

Baer, Will Christopher. Hell's Half Acre. San Francisco: MacAdam/Cage, 2004. p. 133.

Gavin Pate

Pitching forward, losing balance, knowing momentarily that the world and I were askew, incongruent, destined to collide, run smack into one another, pavement to face, knees to gravel, due to the slipping, due to the undeniable loss of traction that had occurred between me and the earth, the way it had slid out from under me, betrayed my feet, pulled the carpet, shuttered, lunged, and moved—nothing else to do but brace for the worst. I was out of sorts with the gestures normally associated with who I am; things were incorrect, I was incorrect.

Pate, Gavin. <u>The Way To Get Here</u>. Lowell, MA: Bootstrap Press, 2006.

Bill Luoma

After I got off the ferry, I bought a national league ball and walked up Broadway. I bit the seams when suits walked by. This raises them up and makes it easier to throw curves.

Luoma, Bill. "My Trip to New York City". <u>Works & Days</u>. West Stockbridge, MA: Hard Press / The Figures, 1998. p. 24.

Andrew Schelling

Clemens pitch'd well. The ballgame was done. Driving away—windy stars & dark cliffs—I saw plutonium in obsolete buildings—deadly long after the glaciers come back, carve up these mountains, go north again.

Schelling, Andrew. "I Stopt in to Watch the Yankees". <u>Tea Shack Interior: New & Selected Poetry</u>. Jersey City: Talisman House, Publishers, 2002. p. 123.

Wally Hedrick

Have I ever talked about the softball games there used to be? There was this tradition for the figurative painters—they were called the Figs—to play the Creepy Crawlers—who were the abstract-expressionists—every year to see who was better…. Each group would come up with a team, and I would be the umpire. I'm very proud of the fact that they would trust me. I mean I had nothing to do with (either style) and the fact was that they recognized that and knew I wouldn't be for one side or another. I don't know what that means, but I like the idea.

Solnit, Rebecca. Secret Exhibition: six california artists of the cold war era. San Francisco: City Lights Books, 1990. p. 114.

David Michalski

Since socialization is never complete and the contents it internalizes face continuing threats to their subjective reality, every society must develop procedures of reality maintenance to safeguard a measure of symmetry between objective and subjective reality.

Michalski, David. "Chthonic Driveway" <u>Cosmos and Damian; A World Trade Center Collage</u>. Lowell, MA: Bootstrap Productions, 2005. p. 139.

Henry David Thoreau

Our truest life is when we are in dreams awake.

Thoreau, Henry David. <u>A Week on the Concord and Merrimack Rivers</u>. Cambridge, MA: Houghton Mifflin, 1961. p. 316.

James Joyce

. . . O thanks be to the great God I got somebody to give me what I badly wanted to put some heart up into me you've no chances at all in this place. . .

Joyce, James. <u>Ulysses</u>. New York: Vintage International, 1990. p. 742.

Vincent van Gogh

As for me, with my presentiment of a new world, I firmly believe in the possibility of an immense renaissance of art. Whoever believes in this new art will have the tropics for a home.

I have the impression that we ourselves serve as no more than intermediaries. And that only the next generation will succeed in living in peace. Apart from all this, our duties and the possibilities of action for us can become clearer to us only by experience and nothing else.

van Gogh, Vincent. The Complete Letters of Vincent van Gogh. v. 3. Boston: Bullfinch Press, 2000. p. 519

Joanne Kyger

Here I am reading about your trip to India again,
with Gary Snyder and Peter Orlovsky. Period.
Who took cover picture of you three

with smart Himalayan backdrop
The bear?

September 2, 1996

Kyger, Joanne. "Poison Oak for Allen". <u>Again: Poems 1989 – 2000</u>. Albuquerque:
La Alameda Press, 2001. p.102.

Amiri Baraka

My intentions are colors, I'm filled with
color, every tint you think of lends to mine
my mind is full of color, hard muscle streaks,
or soft glow round exactness registration. All earth
heaven things, hell things, in colors circulate
a wild blood train, turns litmus like a bible coat,
describes music falling flying, my criminal darkness,
static fingers, call it art, high above the streetwalkers

Baraka, Amiri. "Western Front". The LeRoi Jones / Amiri Baraka Reader. ed. William
J. Harris. New York: Thunder's Mouth Press, 1991. p. 215.

Anne Waldman

Dear Jack Kerouac
who'd rather die than be famous
who ran away from college in 1941
into Memorial cello time
& spilt his gut
50 pesos
Aztec blues
A vast cavern, eh?
I caught (he did) a cold from the sun
upside-down language
ulathamsi Bre-hack! Brop?
Of the cloud-mopped afternoon

and turn this lady upside down

Waldman, Anne. <u>Iovis</u>. Minneapolis: Coffee House Press, 1993. p. 271.

Jean-Michel Basquiat

My subject matters are royalty, heroism, and the streets.

Basquiat, Jean-Michel. Basquiat. Milano: Edizioni Charta, 1999. p. 80.

Stan Brakhage

Because, the lyric cinema that I re-invented, powerfully includes the emotions of the maker, as *literal motion*. So that if I'm all a-tremble, that tremble is being transferred along the line of my arms to the camera, to the film itself, that's recording. If I stumble, that stumble is a set of tumbling rhythms within the frame that's being recorded as I breathe.

Brakhage, Stan. <u>Literal Motion</u>. ed. Christopher Luna. Boulder: Bootstrap Press, 2001. p. 29.

Ryan Gallagher

…memory. The lady who is knitting says her husband's family are all pilots and the lady who has spotted the Elk that she is now sure is an Elk is pointing at her husband as he walks into the viewing car screaming An American Bald Eagle and you missed it and she says You missed An American Bald Eagle and points at the man who had pointed the eagle out to her creating near hysteria, and this keeps going on so I offer to buy Derek a beer if he yells out Look, a mountain lion, (Pause) and it's eating a Baby! But I don't think he will, and Danny, the Elk Lady's son says the person with the most toys wins and Elk Lady says no silly, it's kids, and she asks what time it is…

Gallagher, Ryan. "Dear Andy". Plum Smash and Other Flashbulbs: Letters, Sketches, and Poems 2000-2001. Lowell, MA: Bootstrap Press, 2005. p. 51.

Rebecca Solnit

Roads are not only the major accomplishment of the American spirit of manifest destiny but also its principal expression. Roads are evidence of dissatisfaction, and America was founded upon that quality, upon the belief that there was better than *here*, that problems could be run away from, that freedom was geographical, that being swallowed by the snake will set us free.

Solnit, Rebecca. <u>As Eve Said to the Serpent: On Landscape, Gender, and Art</u>. Athens: The University of Georgia Press, 2001. p. 185.

Gary Snyder

I cannot remember things I once read
A few friends, but they are in cities.
Drinking cold snow-water from a tin cup
Looking down for miles
Through high still air.

Snyder, Gary. "Mid-August at Sourdough Mountain Lookout". The Gary Snyder Reader; Prose, Poetry and Translations 1952 - 1998. Washington, D.C.: Counterpoint, 1999. p. 399.

Ian Hamilton Finlay

In the whole of philosophy there is almost no weather.

Gillanders, Robin. Little Sparta: A Portrait of a Garden. Scottish National Portrait Gallery, 1998.

Tom Morgan

The Next 95 Years

I'm just going to put this out there: This century's most important story is the weather. All other plots, characters, narrative arcs pale in comparison. Apologies to postmodernism for my single pointed perspective.

2005-10-25   14:53:00

Morgan, Tom. On / Going. <http://www.livejournal.com/users/tomorgan/19914.html>.

Tom Raworth

this is the moment
my shadow is thrown on air

Raworth, Tom. "Writers / Riders / Rioters". <u>Moving</u>. London: Cape Goliard Press, 1971.

Tom Waits

take the spokes from your wheelchair
and a magpie's wings
and tie 'em to your shoulders and your feet
i'll steal a hacksaw from my dad
and cut the braces off your legs
and we'll bury them tonight in the cornfield

Waits, Tom. "Kentucky Avenue". <u>Blue Valentine</u>. Elektra, 1978.

Jack Kerouac

A damned lunatic's dream—(un maudit reve de fou)—is life.

Kerouac, Jack. <u>Some of the Dharma</u>. New York: Viking Penguin, 1997. p. 281.

Friedrich Nietzsche

We can comprehend only a world that we ourselves have made.

Nietzsche, Friedrich. <u>The Will to Power</u>. trans. Walter Kaufmann and R.J. Hollingdale. New York: Vintage Books, 1968. p. 272.

Bob Dylan

There's only one step down from here, baby
It's called the land of permanent bliss

Dylan, Bob. "Sweetheart Like You". <u>Bob Dylan, Lyrics 1962-2001</u>. New York: Simon and Schuster, 2004. pp. 465-466.

Ernest Hemingway

You have it now and that is all your whole life is, now. There is neither yesterday, certainly nor is there any tomorrow. How old must you be before you know that? There is only now and if now is only two days, then two days is your life and everything in it will be in proportion. This is how you live a life in two days. And if you stop complaining and asking for what you will never get, you will have a good life. A good life is not measured by any biblical span. So now do not worry, take what you have, and do your work and you will have a long life and a very merry one.

Hemingway, Ernest. <u>For Whom The Bell Tolls</u>. New York: Scribner, 1996. p. 154.

Lucian Freud

A moment of complete happiness never occurs in the creation of a work of art.

Freud, Lucian. "Some Thoughts on Painting (1954)". Theories and Documents of Contemporary Art: A Sourcebook of Artists' Writings. ed. Kristine Stiles & Peter Selz. Berkeley: The University of California Press, 1996. p.221.

Andy Warhol

Before I was shot, I always thought that I was more half-there than all-there—I always suspected that I was watching TV instead of living life. People sometimes say that the way things happen in the movies is unreal, but actually it's the way things happen to you in life that's unreal. The movies make emotions look so strong and real, whereas when things really do happen to you, it's like watching television—you don't feel anything.

Warhol, Andy. The Philosophy of Andy Warhol. New York: Hardcourt Brace, 1975. p. 91.

Walt Whitman

Produce great Persons, the rest follows.

Whitman, Walt. "By Blue Ontario's Shore". <u>Leaves of Grass</u>. New York: Random House, Inc., 1993. p.424.

David Hockney

Portraits aren't just made up of drawing, they are made up of other insights as well.

Hockney, David. <u>David Hockney: Travels with Pen, Pencil and Ink</u>. London: Petersburg Press, 1978.

Joseph Beuys

My objects are to be seen as stimulants for the transformation of the idea of sculpture, or of art in general. They should provoke thoughts about what sculpture *can* be and how the concept of sculpting can be extended to the invisible materials used by everyone:

Thinking Forms	how we mould our thoughts or
Spoken Forms—	how we shape our thoughts into words or
Social Structure—	how we mould and shape the world in which we live: *Sculpture as an* evolutionary process *everyone an artist.*

Beuys, Joseph. "Untitled Statement (c. 1973)". <u>Theories and Documents of Contemporary Art: A Sourcebook of Artists' Writings</u>. ed. Kristine Stiles & Peter Selz. Berkeley: The University of California Press, 1996. pp. 633-34.

Laurie Anderson

I think often the case is that words are just hanging around and I don't really know what to do with them, I can't quite throw them away yet. I always try to start things differently, sometimes with music, sometimes with an image. But I'd say the main focus of it is really words.

Anderson, Laurie. "Interview with Charles Amirkhanian (1984)". Theories and Documents of Contemporary Art: A Sourcebook of Artists' Writings. ed. Kristine Stiles & Peter Selz. Berkeley: The University of California Press, 1996. p. 423.

Jeff Wall

This archaism of water, of liquid chemicals, connects photography to the past, to time, in an important way.

Wall, Jeff. <u>Jeff Wall</u>. London: Phaidon Press Limited, 1996. p. 90.

Ralph Waldo Emerson

Dream delivers us to dream, and there is no end to illusion. Life is a train of moods like a string of beads, and as we pass through them they prove to be many-colored lenses which paint the world with their own hue, and each shows only what lies in its focus.

Emerson, Ralph Waldo. "Experience". Essays of Ralph Waldo Emerson. New York: A.S. Barnes & Company, 1940. p. 143.

George Herms

I'm doing
what   you
are reading
about.

Love GH

Herms, George. I'm doing what you are reading about. Felt pen on paper, 11 x 8 ½ inches. 1982. Los Angeles: Tobey C. Moss Gallery.

John Wieners

Raymond Foye: Do you have a theory of poetics?

John Wieners: I try to write the most embarrassing thing I can think of.

Wieners, John. <u>Cultural Affairs in Boston</u>. ed. Raymond Foye. Santa Rosa, CA: Black Sparrow Press, 1988. p.15.

Andrew Chapman

Shut up, baby.

Chapman, Andrew. "From multiple conversations with the author". Cincinnati: Various locations, 1992-1997.

Laura Akeson-Chapman

Doing a little painting and writing when I can. Perhaps some day you'll see my fictional autobiography—something like *Bridget Jones* meets *Fahrenheit 451*, but about the furniture industry.

Akeson-Chapman, Laura. <u>Christmas Letter 2005</u>. Knoxville: Home printer, 2005.

James Schuyler

The clouds are tinted
gray and violet and shred
the blue in other blues.
Each weed as you walk
becomes a rarity.

Schuyler, James. "A Vermont Diary". <u>Collected Poems</u>. New York: The Noonday Press, 1993.

Klaus Kinski

I feel the jungle coming nearer, the animals, the plants, which have been watching us for a long while without showing themselves. For the first time in my life I have no past. The present is so powerful that it snuffs out all bygones. I know that I'm free, truly free. I am the bird that has managed to break out of its cage—that spreads its wings and soars into the sky. I take part in the universe.

Kinski, Klaus. Kinski Uncut: The Autobiography of Klaus Kinski. trans. Joachim Neugroschel. New York: Viking Adult, 1996.

Walter Benjamin

In every true work of art there is a place where, for one who removes there, it blows cool like the wind of a coming dawn.

Benjamin, Walter. "N [On the Theory of Knowledge, Theory of Progress]". The Arcades Project. trans. Howard Eiland and Kevin McLaughlin. Cambridge: The Belknap Press, 1999. p.474.

Sigmund Freud

The enjoyment of beauty has a peculiar, mildly intoxicating quality of feeling. Beauty has no obvious use; nor is there any clear cultural necessity for it. Yet civilization could not do without it.

Freud, Sigmund. <u>Civilization and Its Discontents</u>. New York: W.W. Norton & Company, 1961. p. 33.

Jacques Derrida

The origin of the artist is the work of art, the origin of the work of art is the artist, "neither is without the other."

Derrida, Jacques. The Truth In Painting. trans. Geoff Bennington & Ian McLeod. Chicago: The University of Chicago Press, 1987. pp. 31-32.

Alfred North Whitehead

But, of course, there is no meaning to 'creativity' apart from its 'creatures,' and no meaning to 'God' apart from the 'creativity' and the 'temporal creatures,' and no meaning to the 'temporal creatures' apart from 'creativity' and 'God.'

Whitehead, Alfred North. <u>Process and Reality</u>. ed. David Ray Griffin & Donald W. Sherburne. New York: The Free Press, 1978. p. 225.

Wallace Berman

Art is Love is God.

Berman, Wallace. <u>Untitled</u>. Box with Bullet, 15 x 13 x 18 cm. Date Unknown. Collection of Temple of Man, Venice.

Max Ernst

Crime ou miracle : un homme complet.
(Crime or miracle: a complete man.)

Ersnt, Max. La femme 100 tetes (The Hundred Headless Woman). trans. Dorothea Tanning. New York: George Braziller, Inc., 1981. pp. 14-15.

Ezra Pound

I have tried to write Paradise

Do not move
    Let the wind speak
        that is paradise.

Let the Gods forgive what I
        have made
Let those I love try to forgive
        what I have made.

Pound, Ezra. <u>The Cantos</u>. New York: New Directions Books, 1995. p. 822.

Edward Dorn

So we somewhat stagger together
down the street, heads down

Dorn, Edward. "Song". <u>The Collected Poems 1965 – 1974</u>. Bolinas, CA: Four Season Foundation, 1975. p. 134.

Thomas Evans

flecks of red plastic shine on painted clay
blanket of reflection means not to be known
only juice going down, in lumps swallowed
melted rags slept by the line of water
having washed away my head with black soap
sporadic throbs housed by a lit recess
make clear the purpose of the letter

Evans, Thomas. "Dutch Space Painting". Onedit: Issue 3. <http://www.onedit.net/issue3/thom/2.html>.

Joseph Cornell

You know, I was thinking, I wish I hadn't been so reserved.

Joseph Cornell's last words to his sister Betty on the telephone the morning he died.

Soloman, Deborah. <u>Utopia Parkway; The Life and Work of Joseph Cornell</u>. London: Pimlico, 1997. p. 372.

Edward Kienholz

I always thought that art should be an easier experience than what it is. Like I can't imagine going into The Louvre and standing in front of a painting and having a vicarious experience with this painting or that artist. It's too pristine; it's too properly hung; it's too perfect...

Pincus, Robert. On A Scale That Competes With The World: The Art Of Edward And Nancy Reddin Kienholz. Berkeley: University of California Press, 1990. p. 48.

Bruce Conner

A rewarding experience for me is a narrative structure where you are not told what to think and what to do. Otherwise, that's what you get in jail. That's what you get with government. And when you get it in art, it can put you to sleep.

Boswell, Peter, Bruce Jenkins, and Joan Rothfuss. <u>2000 BC: The Bruce Conner Story Part II</u>. Minneapolis: Walker Art Center, 1999. p. 31.

Robert Rauschenberg

When someone close to you has been away it's only in about the first fifteen minutes that you're back together that you notice how he has changed from the idea you have of the way he looks. The same thing happens to a painting: when it becomes so familiar that one recognizes it without looking at it, the work has turned into a facsimile of itself. If you do work with known quantities—making puns or dealing with your material—you are shortening the life of the work. It is already leading someone else's life instead of its own.

From an interview with Suzi Gablik in 1968.

Joseph, Branden W. <u>Random Order: Robert Rauschenberg and the Neo-Avant-Garde</u>. Cambridge: The MIT Press, 2003. pp. 261-262.

Larry Clark

In my work, when I really think I've gone too far, when I'm really uncomfortable and don't think anybody will ever speak to me again I know I'm probably ready. I'm there. How far will you go?

Phillips, Lisa. "Richard Prince Interviewed by Larry Clark". <u>Richard Prince</u>. New York: Whitney Museum of American Art, 1992. p. 131.

William S. Burroughs

What do artists do?
They dream for other people.

Burroughs, William S. "The Creative Observer". <u>Painting and Guns</u>. New York: Hanuman Books, 1992. p. 46.

Jane Alden Stevens

Do you love your art enough to destroy it?

Stevens, Jane Alden. "From Class Lecture". Cincinnati: DAAP, 1997.

John Cage

We talk, moving from one idea to another as though we were hunters.

Cage, John. A Year from Monday: New Lectures and Writings. Middletown: Wesleyan University Press, 1967. p. 160.

Robert Mapplethorpe

At some point, I picked up a camera and started taking erotic pictures—so that I would have the right raw material and it would be more mine, instead of using other people's pictures. That was why I went into photography. It wasn't to take a pure photographic image, it was just to be able to work with more images.

Mapplethorpe, Robert. "Interview with Janet Kardon (1988)". Theories and Documents of Contemporary Art: A Sourcebook of Artists' Writings. ed. Kristine Stiles & Peter Selz. Berkeley: The University of California Press, 1996. p.274.

Lenny Bruce

If Jesus had been killed twenty years ago, Catholic school children would be wearing little electric chairs around their necks instead of crosses.

Jim Dine

It's not that technique is nothing to me. It's like this, I've got this little flame. I try to keep it alive and I'm afraid of losing it always. Sometimes technology frightens me. I don't want to fuck with the flame any more than I have to.

Dine, Jim. The Photographs, So Far (Text). Catalogue raisonne by Stephanie Wiles. Gottingen: Steidl Publishers, 2003. p.31.

Yves Tanguy

I believe there is little to gain by exchanging opinions with other artists concerning either the ideology of art or technical methods. Very much alone in my work, I am almost jealous of it. Geography has no bearing on it, nor have the interests of the community in which I work.

Ashbery, John. "Tanguy: The Geometer of Dreams". <u>Yves Tanguy</u>. New York: Acquavella Galleries, Inc., 1974. p. 8.

Henri Matisse

I am unable to make any distinction between the feeling I get from life and the way I translate that feeling into painting.

Tyler Doherty

Instead of emptying
dish rack
gingerly stack more
pots pans bowls
ladles lids glasses
and mugs atop
slick mess nitro-glycerin
steady hand
haphazard soupspoon spire
broadcasting suds

23:VI:02 (9:26 pm)

Doherty, Tyler. <u>Bodhidharma Never Came to Hatboro & Other Poems</u>. Lowell, MA: Bootstrap Press, 2003. p. 43.

Willem de Kooning

It's really absurd to make an image, like a human image, with paint, today, when you think about it, since we have this problem of doing or not doing it. But then all of a sudden it was even more absurd not to do it. So I fear that I have to follow my desires.

de Kooning, Willem. "Content is a Glimpse (1964)". Theories and Documents of Contemporary Art: A Sourcebook of Artists' Writings. ed. Kristine Stiles & Peter Selz. Berkeley: The University of California Press, 1996. p. 197.

Werner Herzog

Film is not analysis, it is the agitation of mind; cinema comes from the country fair and the circus, not from art and academicism.

Herzog, Werner. Herzog on Herzog. ed. Paul Cronin. London: Faber & Faber, 2002.

Alfred Hitchcock

There is no terror in a bang, only in the anticipation of it.

William T. Vollmann

We all know the story of the whore who, finding her China white to be less and less reliable a friend no matter how much of it she injected into her arm, recalled in desperation the phrase "shooting the shit", and so filled the needle with her own watery excrement and pumped it in, producing magnificent abscesses. Less well known is the tale of the man who decided to kill himself by swallowing his athlete's foot medicine. Loving Gloria, he died in inconceivable agony. When they collected a sample of his urine, it melted the plastic cup.—*That*, it is safe to say, is despair.

Vollmann, William T.. <u>Whores for Gloria</u>. New York: Pantheon Books, 1991. p. 1.

Pablo Picasso

Respond in kind and with a million thanks and fond farewells your faithful servant who does lick your boot straps and who squashes in his hand the fattest and most smelly bedbug of them all.

Picasso, Pablo. The Burial of the Count of Orgaz & other poems. ed. and trans. Jerome Rothenberg and Pierre Joris. Cambridge, MA: Exact Change, 2004. pp. 19-20.

Hunter S. Thompson

I came to know gunfire and panic and the sight of my own blood on the streets. I knew every airport in the country before they had metal-detectors & you could still smoke on planes. Pilots knew me by name and stewardesses took me home when my flights were grounded by snow. I made many new friends & many powerful enemies from coast to coast. I went without sleep for seventy or eighty hours at a time & wrote five thousand words in one sitting. It was a brutal life, and I loved it.

Thompson, Hunter S.. <u>Fear and Loathing in America: The Brutal Odyssey of an Outlaw Journalist, 1968-1976</u>. ed. Douglas Brinkley. New York: Simon & Schuster, 2000. p. xxiv.

But really, everything interested me.
                              Max Ernst

The author with Robert Downey Jr.

Derek Fenner was born in Lexington, Kentucky in 1973. He now resides in historic Union Square, Somerville, MA. He is an artist and writer. He is a graduate of the Kerouac School of Disembodied Poetics and his favorite color really is red.

BOOTSTRAP IS . . .

Bootstrap Productions is a 501 (c) 3 non-profit publishing company that promotes the integration of multi-dimensional art forms and experiments into fine press publishing.

The organization seeks to introduce the general public to experimental and contemporary art and writing; to stimulate public interest in the work of new, struggling and relatively unknown artists; and to benefit the community generally by promoting the appreciation of contemporary art and writing.

The organization's goal is to provide a venue that affords the benefits and aesthetics of a quality small press to committed and brilliant writers, visual artists, and musicians who may not otherwise have the opportunity and freedom to display their work as they envision it.

The organization creates the opportunity for the public to experience and learn about such art and writing that might otherwise never have a public forum.

My Favorite Color is Red: Experiments in Lines: 1999-2005 was printed Winter 2006 in an edition of 1000 copies by McNaughton & Gunn of Saline, Michigan, of which 26 are signed and lettered A-Z by the author.

Afterward: Alternate Blurbs
by Gavin Pate

The distinct possibilities of totalitarianism seem no longer to be respected. Fenner is a ruthless pain in the ass. Don't let him tell you differently.

What we have here is a case of overreaching arrogance, BIG-BALLS as they say in those Texas roadhouses...a real case of psychological damage...a guy not quite sure of his ins and outs. The unrealized majesty of misogyny lies in its ability to arouse. So it is with this, and other things.

Let us deceive, cheat, lie the way we've been taught to, with all the viscous cunning the world bequeaths us. Take this book, burn it in a rusted can with the rest of today's priceless ambitions, and at least have the decency to enjoy this, will you?